Frontis: masked lovebird, *A. personata.*

GEORG A. RADTKE

The T.F.H. Book of
LOVEBIRDS

t.f.h.

Front and back covers, endpapers. Left to right, top row: masked (blue), Fischer's, masked, gray-headed (male), Abyssinian (male), peach-faced, masked. Bottom row: peach-faced, Fischer's, masked (blue-white), masked (blue), peach-faced (blue), Abyssinian (female).

Originally published in German by Franckh'sche Verlagshandlung, W. Keller & Co., Stuttgart/1981 under the title *Unzertrennliche (Agaporniden) Haltung, Zucht und Farbspielarten*. First edition © 1981 by Franckh'sche Verlagshandlung, W. Keller & Co., Stuttgart.
© 1981 by T.F.H. Publications, Inc. Ltd. for English translation. A considerable amount of additional new material has been added to the literal German-English translation, including but not limited to additional photographs. Copyright is also claimed for this new material.

119632

Translated by Annemarie Lambrich

Distributed in the U.S. by T.F.H. Publications, Inc., 211 West Sylvania Avenue, PO Box 427, Neptune, NJ 07753; in England by T.F.H. (Gt. Britain) Ltd., 13 Nutley Lane, Reigate, Surrey; in Canada to the pet trade by Rolf C. Hagen Ltd., 3225 Sartelon Street, Montreal 382, Quebec; in Canada to the book trade by H & L Pet Supplies, Inc., 27 Kingston Crescent, Kitchener, Ontario N28 2T6; in Southeast Asia by Y.W. Ong, 9 Lorong 36 Geylang, Singapore 14; in Australia and the South Pacific by Pet Imports Pty. Ltd., P.O. Box 149, Brookvale 2100, N.S.W. Australia; in South Africa by Valid Agencies, P.O. Box 51901, Randburg 2125 South Africa. Published by T.F.H. Publications, Inc., Ltd., the British Crown Colony of Hong Kong.

Contents

Introduction...9

Lovebirds With White Eye Rings........................13

   Masked Lovebird, *Agapornis personata*..................17

   Fischer's Lovebird, *Agapornis fischeri*.....................31

   Nyasa Lovebird, *Agapornis lilianae*.......................35

   Black-cheeked Lovebird, *Agapornis nigrigenis*..............39

Lovebirds Without White Eye Rings.....................41

   Peach-faced Lovebird, *Agapornis roseicollis*...............43

   Red-faced Lovebird, *Agapornis pullaria*...................57

   Abyssinian Lovebird, *Agapornis taranta*...................63

   Gray-headed Lovebird, *Agapornis cana*....................69

   Black-collared Lovebird, *Agapornis swinderniana*..........75

Index...77

Photography

DR. HERBERT R. AXELROD: 15 (top), 25, 29, 41 (top), 46, 48, 49, 51, 55, 61. S. BISCHOFF: 8, 15 (top), 23 (right), 43, 47 (bottom), 52, 59 (bottom), 76. W. DE GRAHL: 22, 39, 40 (bottom), 53, 54, 59, (top). HARRY V. LACEY: 33, 42. A. J. MOBBS: 58. FRITZ PRENZEL: 41 (bottom). H. REINHARD: Endpapers, frontis, 12-13, 16, 19, 20, 26-27, 30, 34, 44, 45, 50, 62, 64, 68. COURTESY OF SAN DIEGO ZOO: 37, 38, 56, 71. TONY SILVA: 23 (left). A. VAN DEN NIEUWENHUIZEN: 24. LOUISE VAN DER MEID: 47 (top). COURTESY OF VOGELPARK WALSRODE: 31, 40 (top), 75. DR. MATTHEW VRIENDS: 65, 66, 70, 72, 73.

The African savannah, habitat of many lovebird species. Opposite: 1. peach-faced (pastel-blue), 2. peach-faced (lutino), 3. black-cheeked, 4. Abyssinian (male), 5. peach-faced (pied yellow-green), 6. masked (blue), 7. masked, 8. Nyasa.

Introduction

Lovebirds are small parrots, about five to seven inches tall. The nine known species *(Agapornis cana, A. fischeri, A. lilianae, A. nigrigenis, A. personata, A. pullaria, A. roseicollis, A. swinderniana, A. taranta)* are natives of the savannah south of the Sahara desert in tropical Africa, an area which includes the island of Madagascar.

The name *Agapornis* (lovebird) comes from the Greek *(agapein,* to love; *ornis,* bird) and may well have originated with the first observers of these birds in their natural habitat. Even though these lively dwarf parrots fight on occasion and their life styles may differ from species to species, there is one characteristic they all have in common: they live in pairs all their lives. None will stray beyond calling distance of its mate. Except for breeding periods, lovebirds live together in sociable groups and often swarm in large numbers through the savannah, the fields, and the jungle. They rest in pairs, cuddling against each other. The partners enjoy grooming and feeding each other. "Marital spats" may be occasionally noisy, but almost always of brief duration.

Lovebirds are cavity breeders. In contrast to other cavity breeders, they carry nesting materials into the nesting hole and construct quite elaborate, tube-shaped breeding chambers. Most species select hollow trees for nesting places. Eggs are white—since they are laid in enclosed spaces, they do not require protective coloring. The females take care of most of the incubating, but the males also spend many hours daily in the nests. While the females are incubating, the males feed them from their crops. At night, they too sleep in the nesting cavity. Even when lovebirds are not raising young, knotholes and other protected places are favored for sleeping.

9

Lovebird babies are fed by both parents. Even after the young have left the nest, they continue to be provided with nourishment by their parents. If the hen is incubating a new clutch, the male often continues to feed the fledglings by himself. Mother Nature's table is richly set: seeds of many varieties of grasses, bushes, and trees; buds and seedlings; insects in all stages of their development; fruits and berries. Because of the high level of energy and liveliness of lovebirds, their appetites are usually excellent. Large flocks can cause considerable damage to grainfields and orchards.

Lovebirds need to be near water, as they drink much and love to bathe. Consequently, they seldom fly far from their watering places. Even though their flight is rapid and agile, their short wings keep them from extended flights. In addition, the periodical tropical droughts tend to limit long flights, as all energy and strength are focused on survival. Droughts affect not only the flying habits of the birds but also—and even more—their breeding instincts.

All these facts must be clearly understood before we acquire our first lovebirds, if we want to keep these children of the tropics happy, healthy, and—if possible—breeding. This last is an obligation which we share more and more, in view of our increasingly impoverished environment. Growing numbers of countries regulate or even prohibit the exportation of their native fauna for whatever purposes. Up to the middle of this century, much damage was done, particularly in importing and exporting birds. Today's bird lover has to concentrate above all on breeding, for his own sake and that of others. We no longer have the luxury of unlimited imports. Fortunately for us, our predecessors have borne the greatest burden, sometimes at great financial costs, since lovebirds were first imported at the beginning of the previous century. We owe an excellent summary to Hampe *(Die Unzertrennlichen,* 1957) who collected all available information and experience about the care and breeding early in this century. Since then, lovebirds have increased in popularity; in addition, the long domestication of many species is leading to many very interesting color mutations.

In this book, I am not necessarily following the established systematic arrangement; rather I will begin with those species which are most popular and most easily bred. For added ease in looking up information, I did not lump together care and feeding, diseases, and breeding idiosyncrasies in particular chapters, but distributed this information under the headings of the

1

2

3

4

5

6

7

appropriate species. Where the requirements for several species are quite similar, reference is made to previously mentioned information.

I hope and trust that this handbook will contribute to a closer relationship between bird lovers on one side and the lovable Africans on the other.

Georg A. Radtke

Distribution of the various *Agapornis* species: 1. *A. cana*, 2. *A. pullaria*, 3. *A. taranta*, 4. *A. swinderniana swinderniana*, 5. *A. swinderniana zenkeri*, 6. *A. fischeri*, 7. *A. personata*, 8. *A. lilianae*, 9. *A. nigrigenis*, 10. *A. roseicollis roseicollis*, 11. *A. roseicollis catumbella*.

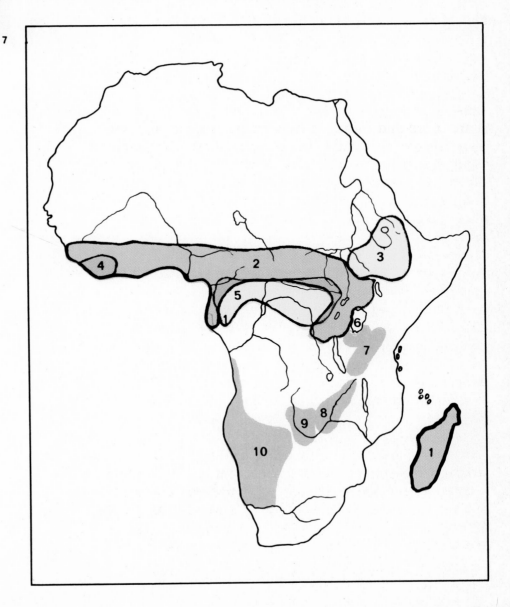

1. gray-headed (male), 2. black-cheeked (yellow), 3. Abyssinian (female), 4. peach-faced (red-flecked), 5. red-faced, 6. black-collared, 7. black-cheeked.

Nyasa lovebirds,
A. lilianae.

Lovebirds With White Eye Rings

In the early days of raising and breeding lovebirds, there was a widespread conviction that the four species with white eye rings *(Agapornis fischeri, A. lilianae, A. nigrigenis, A. personata*—which all belong to the same group) were the easiest to keep and to breed. Further developments have shown that this is not necessarily true, or the numbers of these four species would logically be the greatest. A look at the map of their ranges shows how closely they lie together, indicating a relationship on a geographical basis. It is interesting to note that the species do not interbreed in the border regions, as happens frequently with other birds (like the carrion and hooded crows along the Elbe river or many Australasian weaver finches). The simplest explanation for this is that the natural barriers found in the widely divergent African landscape of jungles, streams, and mountain ranges are formidable obstacles for the short wings of our little parrots. Of course, this no longer applies in their European refuge, the aviaries of the breeders. There the natural barriers are completely absent, as is the need for a daily struggle for food. Different species are deliberately brought into contact with each other, even though they may not have been acquainted before. The natural result has been interbreeding, with fertile offspring. These initially playful attempts of many amateur breeders have proven that the relationship between many species is indeed a close one, and that in many cases their development in separate directions may have been the result of geological upheavals.

To bring the species together again and to raise differently colored offspring may be quite attractive, but it may also result in an undefinable population mix, which theoretically may be quite similar to the original form. There are several examples of this in the history of animal breeding, designated by the term *atavism*. For the amateur breeder, this is of little importance, but it is diametrically opposed to the essential preservation of each species, toward which efforts are so vital today. With this in mind, the two largest German breeders' associations have removed lovebird hybrids from their classification system. Besides, the hybrid of a masked lovebird and a Fischer's lovebird is never as attractive as either of the pure species. In addition, it resembles the black-cheeked lovebird so closely that novices in the field could easily be deceived. Admittedly, the offspring of crosses between black-cheeked lovebirds with Nyasa lovebirds are very attractive, but the low numbers of pure-bred birds of these species prohibit this kind of manipulation. Crossbreeding is justified only if no partners of the same species are available and then the offspring must be declared to be a hybrid.

The four species with white eye rings differ only minimally from each other in their life styles and behavior. For instance, they all tend to carry the nesting materials in their bills; in captivity, they enjoy fresh willow twigs which they quickly split and interweave. Their nests are usually quite solid. Even in an enclosed nesting box, they do not forego a "roof," and the entrance to the nest is near the rear wall.

All in all, the species with white eye rings are less demanding and better adapted to a northern climate than the species without white eye rings. (For exceptions, please see the sections for particular species.)

The peach-faced lovebirds in this aviary have a hollow log available for nesting.

Box cage with gates for feeding on the lower portion of the front.

Wooden nest box suitable for most lovebird species.

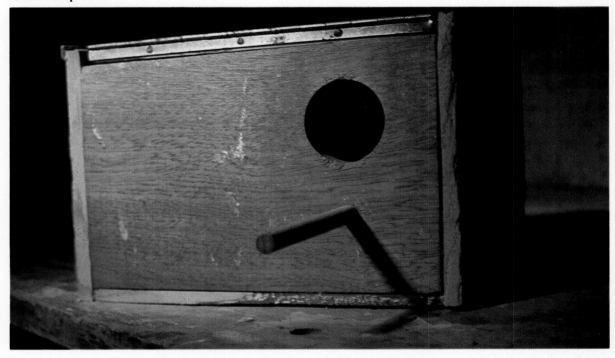

Above and opposite: masked lovebird, *A. personata.*

Masked Lovebird
Agapornis personata

Beyond a doubt, masked lovebirds are the most attractive members of the genus due to their distinctive markings and coloring. Males and females look almost identical and measure about five and three-quarters inches.

According to Forshaw *(Parrots of the World,* T.F.H. Publications, 1977) masked lovebirds live in grassy steppes interspersed with baobab trees and acacias, at altitudes of up to 5,000 feet. They breed in colonies, from March to August. Preferred nesting cavities are the knotholes of baobab trees, but the birds will nest in holes in walls, and even in abandoned swifts' nests. The females rarely lay clutches of more than four eggs. Masked lovebirds feed principally on the seeds of grasses and herbs, which they also pick off the ground while walking rapidly. Their flight is straight and quick, but not of long duration.

In captivity, a pair of masked lovebirds will be satisfied with a cage of about 32 by 16 inches, either all metal wire or a box cage of plastic. (A box cage is a simple box of wood, metal, or plastic, with wire mesh on the longest side.) Wooden cages are not very suitable for lovebirds, since they prove no match for their strong beaks.

If a metal wire cage is used, a nesting box should be fastened to the outside; with a box cage, it is better to attach the nesting box to the inside, since the birds feel more protected there. Modern plastic breeding cages are commercially available; they feature a door on the side and a board in the upper third on which the nesting boxes can be placed, which permit easy access for control purposes. Roomy parakeet nesting boxes are recommended, 6 by 8 and about 10 inches tall, to allow the lovebirds to build a quite bulky nest. The entrance hole should be positioned in the upper part, to one side. It need not be bigger than 2 inches in diameter—masked lovebirds and related species will adapt it to their needs by gnawing it to the correct size. As always, everything that supports the birds' natural instincts will assist in breeding. This is why easily built wooden nesting boxes are best, even though they are not very durable. Perches on the boxes are not absolutely essential, but having one will facilitate the birds' entrance; also, the male likes to sit on it during the incubation period. Even at other times, the parent birds like to use the nesting box as a place to sleep. It is wise, however, to remove this cozy sleeping place, as the birds tend to become stimulated to more frequent breeding than their constitution can deal with. After two or three succeeding breedings, the nesting box should be removed for several months to give the birds a chance to recover fully and to regain their strength. Without this precaution, their life expectancy is shortened, and the health of each succeeding brood decreases until no viable offspring are produced.

People who keep just one pair of lovebirds as companions in a warm apartment and are not interested in offspring should remove the nesting box altogether. What the birds don't know, they won't miss. Incidentally, for almost all cavity breeders, the nesting box is the strongest trigger for breeding. If it is absent, the hen will rarely lay.

If you are not disturbed by their somewhat shrill cries, you will enjoy these delightful roommates, who can become quite tame and confident if they are allowed free flight through the rooms, adequately supervised. They will soon become very clever, returning regularly to their cage, as long as they are never fed anywhere else. Supervision is necessary for the sake of furniture and drapes. Masked lovebirds also need to be protected from exposure to poisonous houseplants; highly curious, they gnaw at everything. Special treats, such as ears of spray millet or greens, will bring them back to the cage.

Lovebirds hand-raised from a very early age can become extremely tame and friendly, since the normal close attachment to parents and siblings is transferred to the human. A person who likes tame, single birds and is fortunate to obtain a hand-raised specimen should therefore be prepared to assume a great deal of respon-

Two mutations of the masked lovebird: blue-white and greenish-tinged yellow.

A masked lovebird (blue mutation) in flight.

sibility. These charmers are called lovebirds or "inseparables" not by accident, and their need for affection and company, focused on their human, is enormous. Many of these birds even learn to repeat a few words or to whistle. They should not be left alone for any length of time; this makes them suitable only for families in which some member is always home, or for people with lots of free time. Others should not consider getting a lovebird, because lack of company may lead to bad habits such as feather plucking, or even to illness and early death.

From about the third week on, when the quills begin to break through and the babies no longer need quite as much warmth, young masked lovebirds can be fed by hand with a warm millet gruel, to which calcium supplements and vitamins have been added. The little birds learn quickly to accept their food from the end of a small spoon. (Let me explain here that I do not in principle advocate the hand-raising of young birds. However, it happens frequently that breeders are forced into this position through default—for whatever reasons—on the part of the parent birds.)

Masked lovebirds kept in pairs or larger groups are much stronger and more disease-resistant than are singly-kept hand-raised birds, unless gross mistakes are made in their care. They do get occasional colds or upset stomachs. These illnesses are quite quickly and simply healed with appropriate medication, diet (millet spray, oat meal), and warmth (heat lamp). Injuries on feet and legs (from fighting birds who bite each other) normally heal quickly; in the case of inflammations, antibiotic powders and such are indicated. Nails and toes lost to frostbite, bites, or other injuries, however, cannot be replaced! Lovebirds seem to have a tendency towards this type of injury because of their fleshy feet, which they injure not only in fights with rival birds, but by hanging on the aviary mesh during periods of frost. For this reason alone, lovebirds should be kept in temperatures well above freezing, although a mild frost is otherwise not harmful to them. The ideal environment is an aviary setting with large frost-free rooms that can be closed off. (In northern climates, these protected rooms should be larger than the outdoor flight areas.) Access to the outdoor sections should be by means of hatches, easily opened or closed according to weather and temperature. In such large enclosures several pairs of masked lovebirds can be permitted to breed at once.

These guidelines should be followed when breeding lovebirds in captivity: (1) Use only true pairs. (2) Do not keep more than one pair per cubic yard. (3) Provide more nesting boxes than couples, with all boxes of the same size and attached at the same level in the upper third of the enclosed room, in such a manner that they can easily be monitored without disturbing the breeding birds.

With such an installation, much enjoyment and breeding success will be assured. You will be able to watch the birds display their charms—caressing, fighting, scolding and chasing each other, and in the next moment sharing food and bath.

Food and water containers should be sufficiently large and numerous. Water dishes will also be used for bathing and, therefore, should be rather shallow, but wide. As all dishes should be positioned so that they will not be soiled from the perches, feeding boards on the insides of doors are particularly handy. Even easier to care for are automatic containers for water and food. Make sure that only completely dry seed is used, as they clog easily. Automatic dishes must be cleaned and checked frequently, and an additional bathing dish will be needed. Cuttlebone and mineral blocks, both essential for the calcium requirements of lovebirds, are easily fastened to the mesh with wire. Galvanized spot-welded wire mesh seems most suitable (see Enehjelm, *Cages and Aviaries,* T.F.H. Publications, 1981.)

In order to give the birds sufficient room for flight, not too many perches should be installed. If at all possible, perches should be of various diameters in order to exercise the birds' feet and their leg muscles. A "climbing tree"—for instance, the lopped-off crown of a dwarf fruit tree with many twigs and branches—is a most welcome opportunity for exercise, climbing, and gnawing. (When you keep lovebirds, you had better get used to the idea that everything made of wood will need to be replaced quite frequently!)

The basic diet consists of good budgerigar mix with a good amount of canary seed, including small striped sunflower seeds and a little hemp, which is augmented according to the season with greens, various weed seeds, half-ripe grass panicles and ears of corn. For breeding birds, we recommend a good commercial nestling food, enriched with mashed egg yolk and grated apples or carrots. Make sure the parrots become used to this diet even before the young are hatched. Not all pairs will accept this kind of food; others prefer crumbled dog biscuits or dog food, fruit, and berries. This is a matter of trial and error, with success the decisive factor, not the means by which it was achieved. Once you have found an acceptable menu, you should stick with it.

Masked lovebird. Some individuals of this species show a strong orange, instead of yellow, coloration on the breast.

For fresh greens, particularly in winter, sprouting the various seeds has proven successful (use a separate dish for each variety). Commercially available sprouting dishes make this simple process partially foolproof. In winter, the drinking water should be enriched at regular intervals by the addition of liquid vitamins. Sick birds may need to be fed one vitamin drop daily in the throat for three successive days, with a plastic eye dropper. This also may prove successful with birds which are reluctant to breed. Once all preparations have been made, the breeding pairs may then move in.

This raises a problem which has caused many a headache among bird lovers: distinguishing the sexes. Many authors cite various external sex distinctions among masked lovebirds and related species, but none has proven completely accurate. Probably the most obvious test is to compare fully-grown birds by size; females of this group of lovebirds are usually larger and heavier—but not without exception. It is fortunate that when the lovebirds can be observed in a group and can be selected accordingly, individual pairs can soon be discerned by their behavior. In a cage, two birds may behave like a pair even though they are of the same sex.

The most accurate method of sexing the birds is by palpation of the pelvic bones from the sternum downward. The pelvic bones of a fully grown male are close together, whereas there is a space of several millimeters between the pelvic bones of a sexually mature female. The use of this method requires a gentle finger tip and practice. The novice should be instructed in its use by an experienced breeder.

Below: peach-faced lovebird nestling.

Below: a clutch of masked lovebird eggs in an opened nest box.

A "dubious" pair should not be put into the aviary, because the imbalance of pairs will cause brood-disturbing fights from the very beginning.

If everything goes according to plan, the pairs should soon begin to build a nest. Both partners are involved in its construction, although it is usually the female who collects the material. You should give the birds a wide choice of nesting materials. Fresh willow twigs are the most suitable; if those are not available, other twigs (of nonpoisonous plants!) will do. Twigs are best put into a sturdy and sufficiently large container filled with water.

Once the nest is ready, the female begins to lay her eggs. They usually lay three to seven eggs at two-day intervals. Incubation lasts from twenty-one to twenty-three days. Many females begin to incubate as soon as the first egg is laid, while others wait for one or two more. Usually, those babies that hatch two days late are just as well taken care of as the others. The young are covered with a pinkish down, which later is replaced by a gray down; this remains until their colorful feathers begin to grow.

Lovebird chicks are hatched blind; they open their eyes on about the tenth day. After about forty-three days, the fledglings leave the nest. Their feathers are fully grown, and even though their plumage is still youthfully pale, it already shows the distinctive markings and coloration of mature birds. Healthy youngsters fly well from the beginning and are quite capable of feeding themselves, but they are fed for a while longer, usually by the male. By this time, the hen is usually busy with her next clutch.

Once the young birds are on their own, an especially careful watch must be kept on the other birds in the aviary. As soon as there are any indications of dangerous biting—just when is unpredictable—the young birds must be separated from the old. This is one reason why a serious breeder of lovebirds cannot make do with one aviary; he needs to have at least two available.

During the warm season, though the young birds need no sleeping boxes, they will be grateful for some boards in the upper third of the protected rooms so that they may rest their still-weak legs while sleeping. For the owner of an outdoor aviary, the best time for breeding is during the warm season. The angle of the sun's rays, the availability of greens, etc., are to his advantage. Winter breeding is successful only in well-heated indoor rooms. Masked lovebirds and related species that winter in cold temperatures should be given sleeping boxes without nesting material and, if possible, should be kept separated according to sex. This will keep the females

Masked lovebird, wild, or normal, coloration.

The blue mutation of the masked lovebird, in which the green is replaced by blue.

from laying. An occasional "lost" egg is no tragedy, even though the health of young females in very cold rooms may be endangered by egg binding. Pairs that have bred two or three times during the summer season should be separated from the breeding colony and kept in a manner similar to young birds.

When breeding masked lovebirds in single pairs in box cages having a minimum length of 40 inches (or better, 50 to 60 inches), many of these problems will be avoided. Perhaps birds used to an aviary will be slower to breed, but breeding will be simpler. Control, individualized feeding, and cleaning are easier. For this reason, many breeders are switching to breeding in separate cages, although more work is involved with this method. The amount of time involved should not be underestimated: it takes time to establish a certain routine. Therefore, it is much better to begin small, with one or two pairs. Those who do not wish too much expense at first will enjoy their hobby more by beginning modestly and growing with the earnings from selling the offspring, reinvesting the money earned and the experience gained.

Especially recommended are large box cages with removable interior partitions. Such cages can easily be adapted as flight cages for the young and resting birds, since lovebirds do not require large outdoor aviaries. Unlike budgerigars and other parakeets, lovebirds do not care much for long-distance flights. This is indicated by their build: short tail and wings. Of course, it is good for young and resting birds to have the opportunity to fly in light, air, and sun, or showering in the rain but it is not absolutely necessary. For this reason, masked lovebirds and similar species can successfully breed in the city, without the availability of outdoor aviaries. All that is needed is a bright, dry basement or attic room that can be adequately lighted (with wide-spectrum fluorescents, for instance), heated (with economical electrical units), and aired (ventilator, hygrometer). Adequate humidity is a must, since lovebird eggs hatch perfectly only in a humidity of 65% or better (hence the hygrometer). The use of water dishes with large surfaces (even aquariums), regular sprinkling of the floor (which is best constructed of easily cleaned concrete), and care for constantly fresh nesting materials will prevent any problems.

Separate cages are an absolute requirement for color-selective breeding, since most species of lovebirds appear to follow the formation of hereditary mutations of parakeets, immensely enriching our hobby!

Left to right, top row: masked (blue), Fischer's, masked, gray-headed (male), Abyssinian (male), peach-faced, masked. Bottom row: peach-faced, Fischer's, masked (blue-white), masked (blue), peach-faced (blue), Abyssinian (female).

The first blue masked lovebirds were bred in England, descending, according to Hampe *(Die Unzertrennlichen,* 1967), from a wild blue captured in Tanganyika in 1927. As was to be expected, this was a recessive trait from the wild green coloring. Thus pure green x blue will result in all green young, independent of sex, which, however, are all split to blue; matings with each other will produce 25% blue offspring. Split-to-blue x blue will bring forth 50% blue. Blue x blue will give 100% blue, since the blues are pure. This allowed them to be bred rather quickly. At this time, they are only slightly more expensive than the green, after which they are certainly the most attractive variety. If blues continue to be bred with blues only, after some generations size will suffer. At this point, or preferably before, healthy wild birds should be bred back into the line. This is the entire secret of these mutations.

Nobody knows exactly when the first yellow appeared. It seems likely that the Japanese were the first to breed them. From there, these birds came to Europe, maybe ten but no longer than twenty years ago. Their color is not pure yellow but faintly suffused with green. Their recessive inheritance follows the same rules as that of the so-called yellow parakeets that have a green tinge. Their masks are not black, but brownish gray, mixed with red, which occasionally leads to their mistaken identification as peach-faced lovebirds. A hybrid of these species, however, never shows this much yellow. The future will tell whether it is possible to obtain a purer yellow, as this mutation is still quite recent.

Once there were blue and yellow birds, the breeding of white masked lovebirds was only one step removed, because just as white, blue-tinged parakeets were bred from blue x yellow, Mendel's laws of heredity lead us to expect one white-blue offspring in sixteen from a blue x yellow pair. These birds are predominantly bluish white, with a light gray head and an almost white beak. With their pastel coloration, they are quite attractive in their way. Since they breed recessively to yellow, it is worthwhile to breed them within the same stock, particularly since these two colors enhance each other.

We also know of masked lovebirds that show a strong orange coloring instead of yellow. Even the head feathers may be underlaid with this color, without necessarily indicating a crossing with a black-cheeked lovebird. Hampe knew about these birds, but he mistakenly identified this coloration as a sign of age. In fact, young birds exhibiting these attractive colors are known today. Since there is no geographical separation between races in the wild, this strong coloration is prob-

Sunflower seeds figure in the diets of all lovebird species. Shown here is a masked lovebird.

ably a result of natural selection. However, it cannot properly be called a direct mutation.

For exhibition, all lovebirds are shown individually in internationally approved budgerigar show cages. The birds are evaluated by qualified judges, according to a prescribed point system, winning places according to quality and, if necessary, size, earning ratings from "satisfactory" to "excellent."

As a proof of breeding standards, [in Germany] birds which are exhibited must be banded. The official diameter of the band is 4.5mm for all lovebirds. This legally required banding is no small problem. For various reasons, banding the birds with closed rings, such as can be obtained through membership in a breeders' association, is the best method. In addition to the breeder's membership number and a running number from 001 on, the information contained on the ring includes the year, so that the bird's age is verifiable throughout its life, whether the bird is exhibited or not. This is always an advantage when buying and selling. Babies banded at an age of ten to twelve days become completely adjusted to the rings, so that they will not attempt to remove them later on. But with open rings, such as the central association of German pet dealers has issued as officially recognized rings for non-organized breeders, there is always the danger of removal of the rings by the birds themselves. Lovebirds, with their strong, clever beaks, are specialists in this—particularly when they were not banded until adult. Many birds will not eat or rest until the ring has been removed and has disappeared somewhere in the sand or grit. This can lead to problems if the birds have already been registered in the official register which every parrot breeder is required to keep and the bird is going to be put up for sale.

Bird shows are also social events between associations, but their main purpose is to increase the quality of breeding. All lovebirds behave quite well during those few days in their separate show cages if they have been accustomed to this since early youth through gradual isolation (after having been lured into the cage by means of some delicacy) and training in solitude, at first for hours, then for days.

Above and opposite: Fischer's lovebird, *A. fischeri.*

Fischer's Lovebird
Agapornis fischeri

The closest relatives of masked lovebirds are Fischer's lovebirds, which are only slightly smaller. Males and females have the same coloration.

The natural habitat of Fischer's lovebirds is northwest of that of the masked lovebirds, separated from it by jungle. They inhabit an area with a very similar ecological structure, although distinguished by slightly more cultivated land.

The voices of *A. fischeri* are louder and more strident than those of masked lovebirds. On the whole, Fischer's tend to be more lively. After the war, the numbers of *A. fischeri* were the fastest to recover, which shows the stamina of the birds. For many years, they were considered to be the best and most reliable breeders. Lately, their popularity suffered somewhat because their colors are not as bright and they do not show the same variety of color mutations as the other species. This is most likely due to the fact that they are not bred as often—but this may change tomorrow. In any case, their numbers in Europe are sufficient to assure a good supply at a reasonable price.

Fischer's lovebirds are very sociable and adaptable in the wild. There are accounts in Forshaw's book of their taking over abandoned weaver nests. Like masked lovebirds, they breed in colonies. Yellow and pied yellow *fischeri* have been bred in Germany for more than fifty years, with the yellow showing a pure, strong color except for the pale pink mask. Unfortunately, they were in the wrong hands. The breeders did not heed the advice of experts and did not breed the yellows with strong green birds; in order to multiply them quickly, they continued to interbreed them. Since the yellows were not strong and viable, they died out before becoming popular. Let this be a lesson to anyone fortunate enough to breed a new mutation (which is certainly within the realm of possibility with lovebirds). When a bird of a new color occurs, some inbreeding will be required because most mutations are recessive, probably requiring mating with a parent or a sibling to fix the new color. However, as soon as there is more than one bird of the new color, strong, vital, fertile natural-colored birds should be crossed with them to prevent the new mutation from dying out. Not by accident do scientists speak of a "loss mutation," in which there is not only a loss of color (lighter shades) but also a loss of other, at first less clearly visible, qualities. If these negative qualities are doubled by inbreeding, a general loss of vitality and fertility will become noticeable, which may even lead to the death of the birds. All of today's apparently viable variations that are based on mutations have slowly and patiently been bred for health and vitality by crossing with the best wild birds, which are the result of nature's own selection. In this manner, we have today once more quite pretty and easily bred yellow and even more yellow-green *fischeri*. According to Rutgers (*Handbook of Foreign Birds,* 1969), there are reports of blues, yet according to the color composition of *A. fischeri*, they cannot be overly attractive as compared to the natural coloration. (See also blue *A. roseicollis.)*

In feeding and care Fischer's lovebirds have very similar requirements to those of masked lovebirds. They appear to be even slightly less susceptible to lower temperatures. However, the danger of frost damage to their feet remains and they, too, should winter in a frost-free area. Because Fischer's lovebirds have a greater tendency toward fighting than *A. personata,* they should be bred only in individual cages. However, breeding is encouraged when two pairs in adjacent cages are able to see and hear each other, even though they may fight occasionally through the bars. Sex determination is very difficult with this species, too. Young and resting birds may be put into frost-free aviaries without nesting boxes, like masked lovebirds.

Unfortunately, breeders and dealers have adopted the bad habit of referring to them as "Fischer's" for the sake of brevity, instead of using the pretty name "peach-headed." According to Hampe, the explorer Reichenow named this species in honor of Dr. G. A. Fischer, with whom he had discovered masked lovebirds and peach-heads on an exploratory voyage.

Fischer's lovebirds.

Above and opposite: Nyasa lovebirds, *A. lilianae*. The birds above appear content on the rough bark.

Nyasa Lovebird
Agapornis lilianae

Nyasa, or Lilian's, lovebirds are the smallest of the species with white eye rings. They measure only four and one-half to five inches in length, and again, males and females are colored alike. Unfortunately, this smallest, one of the most beautiful—and up to now the rarest—eye-ring lovebird has remained in the hands of breeders since its breeding in enclosed conditions in Europe has not been very successful. If we had not been able to obtain occasional imports of wild stock, this species might well have become extinct in our cages and aviaries.

According to Forshaw and Rutgers, their natural habitat is along the humid, wooded banks of the Zambezi River. Here they nest in knotholes of tall trees; they have also nested in the eaves of houses and in the abandoned nests of the buffalo weaver. As nesting materials, they use twigs, straw, and similar materials. They are not very selective in their choice of a nesting place or material. Without a doubt, the high temperatures and humidity in their natural breeding range work in their favor. They are said normally to lay four or five eggs. Breeders here have noticed a large incidence of infertile and dead-in-shell eggs and count themselves lucky to raise two fledglings from each clutch. The incubation period lasts for twenty-one days and begins with the laying of the first egg.

Outside the breeding season, *lilianae* often undertake more extensive group flights than their relatives, in flocks of a hundred birds or more, and they do no little damage to the millet fields. This is one reason why Nyasa lovebirds, even though smaller than the masked, black-cheeked and Fischer's lovebirds are dissatisfied with small cages. Since they are more peaceable than the other three species, they can be raised and bred in groups. De Grahl *(Papageien in Haus und Garten,* 1976) kept four pairs in a not overly large aviary. Under no circumstances should they be exposed to the winter temperatures of Europe, even though they do not require tropical heat.

In addition to the usual grains, they should be fed a lot of greens, fruits, berries, and sprouts. As nestling food, Pinter *(Handbuch der Papageienkunde,* 1979) recommends bread moistened with milk—a good and simple food for many seedeaters. However, we must pay close attention to the absolute freshness of the food; sour milk will turn the best-intentioned feeding too easily into the opposite. Forshaw additionally mentions nectar from eucalyptus blossoms and such as additional nutrition, so it will be no mistake if we offer the blossoms of fruit trees in spring.

In the U.S.A. there exists already a strain of beautiful lutinos (pure yellow with red eyes and mask), but they have reached Europe only in negligible quantities. Pinter also mentions blue *lilianae.* Because of their similarity, breeders need to be cautioned against cross-breeding with *fischeri.* Young birds do not yet show the beautiful red of the head—this is a positive indication of youth. Finally, while Nyasa lovebirds are quite dainty, their voices are most definitely not!

Opposite: Nyasa lovebirds can be offered the blossoms of fruit trees.

Above and opposite: black-cheeked lovebirds, *A. nigrigenis*. Lovebirds as tame as the one shown opposite may be allowed outside of their cages without worry.

Black-Cheeked Lovebird
Agapornis nigrigenis

These especially dainty African dwarf parrots (about five and one-half inches long) are particularly endangered in their purebred form, both in the very small area of their natural habitat and in captivity, in spite of the fact that they are quite reliable breeders once they become used to their environment. Like the *lilianae* they live in the warm, humid climate of wooded river valleys. De Grahl mentions that temperatures of around 60°F. are indicated for fresh imports. They have been known to survive temperatures below freezing, he adds, and in captivity they breed up to three times in succession. The main danger to their survival in the wild, according to Forshaw, is excessive capture and exportation for the bird market. Thus we are called upon to care even more intensively for the purity of the remaining stock.

Many of the birds available for sale are not purebred. No other species of lovebird has had to suffer quite as much as the black-cheeked in regard to indiscriminate mixed breeding. The reasons are evident: their coloration and markings are apparently strongly dominant, they will readily breed with the masked lovebird, and they are much more expensive than the wild-colored masked lovebird. According to de Grahl, purebred black-cheeked lovebirds must show no black head, no pure yellow on the throat, and no blue on the upper tail-coverts.

Their care and feeding are the same as for masked lovebirds. A large common aviary and a colony breeding system of several pairs appear to promise more success. *A. nigrigenis* shares this characteristic with *A. lilianae.* The size of the clutch is three to five eggs, and incubation lasts for twenty-four days. Naturally, from these two species, some quite attractive hybrids have frequently been bred; these unfortunately turn into an unattractive hodge-podge in succeeding generations, neither one nor the other. Since *A. lilianae* also are endangered, at least in Europe, such manipulations should evidently not be undertaken.

Color mutations of the black-cheeked are unknown to date. The appearance of mutations always goes hand in hand with large numbers of domestically bred animals and is, therefore, a result of domestication. But first, more needs to be done for the preservation of the nice and easily kept and bred black-cheeked lovebird. Exhibition of these birds should be undertaken for publicity purposes, because nothing attracts more attention to a good cause than the exhibition of healthy, domestically bred birds to the public.

All the white-eye-ring lovebirds, but particularly the larger, more robust masked and Fischer's are suited to liberty if the situation permits. Whoever lives in a single house surrounded by gardens may risk letting his breeding birds fly free from the garden aviary. It is best to wait until there are babies in the nest, when the tie to the nest is strongest. When a trap door in the roof or upper third of the wire enclosure is opened, one or the other of the breeding pair will explore the surroundings but will not venture beyond calling distance of its mate's voice. Later, the fledglings will quickly and skillfully become accustomed to going in and out, and the entire flock will participate in excursions through the neighborhood, always returning to the feed dishes, even though many delicacies can be found outside. (Since buds, shoots, and fruit are favored tidbits, watch out for trouble with the neighbors!) From October, at the latest, through April the door to the outside world should remain closed. If permitted constant liberty, lovebirds rarely leave the area, but they tend to build nests in the eaves of houses and similar places, revert to the wild, and eventually die in the frost and snow of winter.

Above and below: black-cheeked lovebirds. These individuals show some of the variation in coloration typical of this species.

Differences in eye rings: masked lovebird (above), peach-faced (below).

Lovebirds Without White Eye Rings

The separation of lovebirds into species with and without white eye rings is not completely understandable. Rather, *A. roseicollis,* being closest to the species with eye rings, represents a kind of flowing connection. Moreover, the species without eye rings are nowhere nearly as closely related among themselves as are those with eye rings, all of which are often considered subspecies of *A. personata.* The following five species can be clearly distinguished from one another by habitat, appearance, and behavior. However, they all share a rather peculiar and (for the observer) amusing manner of transporting nesting materials between the feathers on the back and rump, and occasionally on the chest. This is done mostly by the females, who take extraordinary, almost human, pains selecting and rejecting pieces of bark, loading themselves up, losing half of it, reloading, rising to the nesting hole heavily laden, losing half the cargo there, and starting over again. Somehow they manage to build a comfortable nest after all! This is one of their inborn traits which they cannot abandon even in captivity. Many bird lovers like to keep these little parrots mainly because of their amusing nesting habits, putting less value on breeding success. Unfortunately, this is quite irresponsible today, because with the exception of *A. roseicollis,* these species are endangered.

Above and opposite: peach-
faced lovebird, *A. roseicollis.*
The photo above shows the
wild coloration, including the
red spot on the tail feathers.
One of the yellow mutations
is shown opposite; note the
greenish edges on some of
the feathers.

Peach-faced Lovebird
Agapornis roseicollis

This species, which inhabits a comparatively large area, is divided into two subspecies: *A. r. roseicollis* and, in southern Angola, the smaller, more intensely colored *A. r. catumbella*. Both are available in Europe through importation and are often unwittingly interbred. This renders almost insignificant the external sex characteristics cited by Hampe: The female: larger; wider base of beak; wider seat; smaller, rounder head; front paler red. The male: smaller; beak and seat narrower; larger, longer head; front brighter red. As with the four species with eye rings, the most accurate method of sex determination here too are pelvic measurement and observation of behavior. When approached, the female disappears first into the box. Only females will tuck nesting materials between their feathers; young females will do this playfully even before reaching sexual maturity. It is almost exclusively the male that initiates courtship and regurgitates food from his crop.

Peach-faced lovebirds, which are bigger and stronger than the eye-ring species—and also louder—are considered the best adapted, most domesticated, and easiest-to-breed lovebirds. In their native habitat, they live on steep, arid mountain cliffs on the edge of the desert. Here they breed in colonies in rock caves, on buildings, and in abandoned nests of social weavers and stripe-breasted sparrow-weavers. To gather food and drink they undertake long flights daily. In Africa, the breeding time coincides with the rainy season (January to March). At that time, the flocks are only small; outside of the breeding season, however, *roseicollis* may gather by the hundreds and cause considerable damage to crops.

A dilute yellow-green, one of
the color mutations of the
peach-faced lovebird.

The mutation called blue;
here the head of the female is
the more strongly colored.

The first peach-faced lovebirds came to Germany in 1860 and were successfully bred there in 1869. They lay three to five eggs, occasionally six. Incubation lasts from twenty-one to twenty-three days, nestling time five to six weeks; after another two weeks, the young are on their own. The juvenile plumage resembles that of adults, but all the colors are paler. Because of a tendency towards quarreling among peach-faces, and even more so toward other birds, it was believed for a long time that they should be kept and bred as pairs only. Among breeders today cages at least thirty-two inches are considered the minimum. It is possible, however, to breed several pairs of *roseicollis* in a spacious aviary. If the flights are particularly large, the growing young birds can remain there. When breeding in single boxes, to prevent injuries inflicted by the older birds, the fledglings should be removed as soon as they are self-sufficient.

Care and feeding are similar to those of the species with eye rings. We should offer more and larger sunflower seeds, as well as dry or germinated oats and wheat. If we also offer plenty of greens and fruit, a special breeding diet should not be necessary. Many pairs may not even accept it. Young birds are more likely to try out a new diet.

When breeding there occasionally may be difficulties due to the often over-developed nest-building instinct of the species, which may lead to the building of a new nest on top of one in which eggs have already been laid or to abandoning a clutch in favor of beginning the construction of a new nest in another box. Once we become aware of this, spare nesting boxes must be removed after a maximum of three clutches or the pairs must be separated; otherwise, they will continue to breed, which will weaken the female, often leading to her death. In addition, weakened *roseicollis* females easily become eggbound, which is often noticed only when it is too late to save them.

The pink down covering of the newly hatched babies is another indication of the close relationship with the eye-ring species. Peach-faced lovebirds have repeatedly been crossed with masked and Fischer's lovebirds; the offspring exhibited the markings of the *A. roseicollis* but were, as far as they were tested, not fertile.

In the first decades of breeding peach-faced lovebirds, there was a lamentably high incidence of embryos dead in their shells shortly before hatching. This was ascribed to a lack of humidity in the air. Many methods were used to try and improve that situation, from misting the boxes to positioning containers with

A dilute blue peach-faced.

46

The lutino mutation has also appeared in the Nyasa lovebird (below). The bill color most obviously distinguishes mutations of this species from those of the peach-faced lovebirds (above).

moss and sponges below the nests. Since the birds in their homeland nest in very arid areas (at best only the use of rotting nesting materials could possibly increase the humidity within the nest), lack of humidity could not be the only reason for the embryonic deaths. This suspicion has been corroborated by the birds themselves in terms of their adaptation to the European climate. The incidence of unhatched embryos has dropped so drastically that the problem of humidity is rarely discussed any longer. Still, a bone-dry attic room is not suited for the breeding of lovebirds, and care should be taken that the humidity does not go lower than 65%. When, in addition, we see to the availability of fresh willow twigs during the breeding season (de Grahl recommends also lime and birch), this source of danger can be virtually eliminated. Diminishing fertility as a consequence of domestication and occasionally inbreeding is another matter.

In breeding for color mutations, the peach-faced lovebird is second only to the budgerigar in rapid development of divergent colors. This is to be taken literally because today, with only very few exceptions, all the mutations known from the budgerigar can be found in the plumage of the peach-faced lovebird. (In the author's budgerigar books the coloration of the plumage, and its development, structure, and inheritance are treated: *Budgerigars* and *Encyclopedia of Budgerigars,* T.F.H. Publications.)

According to de Grahl, a blue peach-faced lovebird was observed in the wild. In captivity, though, the first mutation (in the fifties) was the dominant pied yellow-green birds. As with a majority of pied variations, this trait can only be called partly dominant. At first, only birds with lighter, flecked heads appeared. When they were paired with each other, their offspring showed a wide pattern variation, with no two birds resembling one another, and the color ranging from predominantly green to predominantly yellow. Today, the pied birds can be considered pure. The international exhibition standard prefers pied peach-faces marked 50:50, with mostly symmetrical markings. These birds have kept the peach mask, which should be pure, as should the blue rump, which is merely shaded toward turquoise. This latter characteristic differentiates the pied birds from the true yellow (in place of which dilute pied birds are occasionally and fraudulently offered for sale).

Many pied green-yellow birds tend to show red-flecked feathers elsewhere than on the mask, but these birds have not shown themselves to be a hereditary variation (de Grahl). Many breeders tend to consider

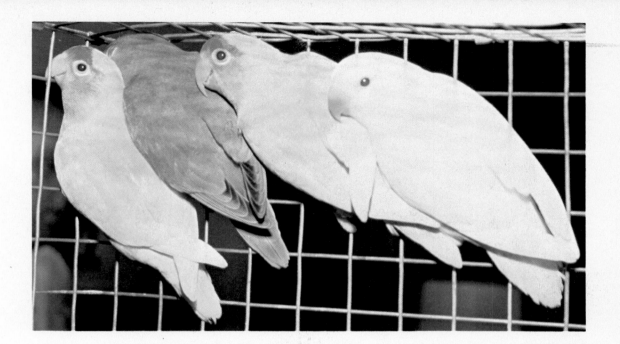

Like the blue, the yellow mutations of peach-faced lovebirds (shown on these pages) can be subject to dilution. The light-colored individuals here are often called albinos.

Above and opposite: peach-faced lovebirds, wild coloration.

this coloration as an indication of some deficiency, since it often appears in older birds or disappears again at the next molt.

One of the most attractive color mutations of *A. roseicollis* is the "Golden Cherry" bred by the Japanese in the late fifties. It shows red and blue on a golden yellow ground with the same intensity as that of wild birds. The blue is merely a little paler, the yellow with a faint greenish tinge. The first *roseicollis* of this variety were exported to Switzerland at a high price. Offspring later came to Holland and Germany. Comparatively good success in breeding has led to somewhat lowered prices, but these birds are still in great demand. The name "Golden Cherry" has been kept in other languages for lack of something better. A little later, the Americans bred a similar mutant which they called "Imperial Cherry Head." It is characteristic of the Swiss sense of simple democracy that these birds are simply called "Yellow-greens" there. One authority accurately calls them "bordered" or "scaled." Indeed, the greenish yellow plumage of these birds shows almost a ghost image outlining the feathers, similar to that of many thinned-down budgie colorations; the large feathers are pale gray, the rump thinned-down blue. The ground color varies from almost yellow to almost green.

Pretty as a picture are the lutino peach-faced lovebirds, which are pure yellow with the exception of the red mask and eyes. All horny parts are of a pale flesh color in this sex-linked mutation. It is recommended to cross lutinos with strong, wild-colored greens to keep them strong and to maintain their coloration.

Cinnamon and dilute varieties have already been bred from *roseicollis*. They have paler colors, lighter horny parts, and brownish wings as characteristics distinguishing them from the wild coloration. Both have reddish eyes as nestlings, but while those of the cinnamon variety darken as they grow older, those of the dilutes remain reddish for life.

Much more importance must be ascribed to the blue strain. As is the case with budgerigars, it is possible to speak of distinct blue and green strains in *A. roseicollis*. As evidenced by the color photographs, the blue peach-faced lovebirds are not really blue, as are blue masked lovebirds, but turquoise or pale yellowish green. So far, the yellow pigment has not been completely removed from *A. roseicollis*. It is merely changed, thinned-down, so to speak, which is equally true of the rose red that remains noticeable on the front of the blues and has not quite disappeared from the delicate gray of their neck

Peach-faced lovebirds: albino and Golden Cherry, with a yellow-green pied, and a blue in the background.

The red flecks in the plumage of this peach-faced lovebird are the result of variations in diet, not an inheritable factor.

feathers. Consequently, pied blue birds, which were easily bred through greens in two generations, are not blue-white, but pied blue-yellow (blue is recessive to green, as in budgerigars). Their coloration strongly resembles that of the pied forms of blue "yellow-faced" budgies and they are called just that by many breeders. It is assumed that most breeders of lovebirds are familiar with the blues for color inheritance in the budgerigar, because the topic of color breeding understandably exceeds the scope of a book dealing only with the species of lovebirds. One authority recommends crossing pied greens with blues, for the enhancement of their coloration. This applies not only for pieds but also for all greens and blues, because it has become a "golden rule" in breeding budgerigars for more than a hundred years: green enhances blue, and vice versa.

Lutinos had to be bred with blues to obtain albinos, which also have a sex-linked inheritance. These are presently available, but because of the incomplete removal of the yellow pigment they cannot be pure white. Rather they are a pale lemon yellow and therefore quite attractive. There are also bordered, cinnamon, and dilute birds from the blue strain in this pale yellow ground color, the creation of which is not difficult if the rules of color selection in budgerigars are followed.

We know also that all color strains of *A. roseicollis* are ruled by the presence or absence of so-called dark factors (Bielfeld, *Handbook of Lovebirds,* T.F.H. Publications). The wild-colored *roseicollis* has no dark factor and is therefore on the same level as the light-green parakeet. The dark-green *roseicollis* has one dark factor and appears noticeably darker (jade) green, with an ultramarine-colored rump. The olive variety, with two dark factors, is of a dull olive color with a dark blue-gray rump, which resembles the shade of the mauve budgerigar. Wild-colored birds (light green without a dark factor) are pure as are the olive variety. Paired among themselves, olives will produce offspring that look like their parents because there can be no more than two factors. Dark greens, however, with one dark factor, are of intermediate inheritance, and their offspring will be divided into 25% light green (wild-colored), 25% olive, and 50% dark green. The same holds true in the blue strain: the common turquoise colored as the "light blue" without a dark factor; the only slightly darker colored "dark blue" (its rump color like that of the dark green) with one dark factor; and the "mauve" (as in the budgerigar) with two dark factors. This bird is lead-colored on its upper side, light gray on the under side, with the mask faintly red. The gray has a very faint red tinge throughout, so that mauve is the absolutely correct name for this coloration. Inheritance is the same as for the different color shades of the greens. As blue factors are recessive to green, all greens split to blue interact with blue according to the presence, absence, or double presence of the dark factor. Here are some examples—the color after the slash (/) indicates the recessive color:

Light-green x light-blue = 100% light-green/blue
Light-green/blue x light-green/blue = 50% light-green/blue,
    25% light-green (pure), 25% light-blue
Light-green/blue x light-blue = 50% light-green/blue,
    50% light-blue
Dark-green/blue x light-blue = 25% light-green/blue,
    25% dark-green/blue, 25% light-blue,
    25% dark-blue
Olive/blue x light-blue = 50% dark-green/blue,
    50% dark-blue
Dark-green/blue x dark-blue = light-green/blue,
    dark-green/blue, olive/blue, light-blue, dark-blue, mauve
Olive/blue x dark-blue = as above, but
    proportionately more olive/blue and mauve
Olive/blue x mauve = 50% olive/blue, 50% mauve
    (since both have two dark factors)

Simpler:
Light-green x light-green = 100% light-green
Olive x olive = 100% olive
Mauve x mauve = 100% mauve

But:
Dark-green x dark-green = 25% light-green, 25% olive,
    50% dark-green
Dark-blue x dark-blue = 25% light-blue, 25% mauve,
    50% dark-blue

Peach-faced lovebird, the lutino mutation.

Of course, the percentages indicated are accurate only with 100 young, and the results may differ from brood to brood. The cited examples can only indicate what to expect from a given pairing. In all these examples sex is of no importance.

Even though peach-faced lovebirds with one or two dark factors may not be as striking in color as the comparable budgerigars, their important role in the breeding of distinctively marked pied mutations that are rich in contrast should not be overlooked, nor should that of the greens for the enhancement of the color of all yellows. Grays are just one step removed from gray-greens through ordinary greens, as in budgerigars. The gray is said to be a muddy gray-blue, with a lighter underside. Gray-winged birds and birds with lighter coloring above and darker underside are said to exist, results of dark-green/blue x dark-green/blue, which show two shades of blue in their plumage. It is not unlikely that the breeding of *A. roseicollis* still has many surprises in store—one more reason to warn against careless, uninformed experiments.

As long as other circumstances are of no consideration, peach-faced lovebirds are particularly suited to liberty. In the bird park at the Hermann Monument in the Teutoburger Forest, an entire flock comes and goes as it pleases, even nesting under the eaves of neighboring frame houses. Its owner had previously gained experience with them in his own garden. They are a sight to be seen!

Peach-faced lovebirds, normal coloration and pied.

Above and opposite: red-faced lovebird, *A. pullaria*.

Red-faced Lovebird
Agapornis pullaria

This particularly colorful and lively dwarf parrot has been Problem Bird Number One among lovebirds. The main reason is probably a lack of adaptability as far as its choice of a nesting site is concerned. Even though the species was discovered in the seventeenth century and imported soon after, and while much printer's ink has been used up in writing about these birds, there is insufficient or even contradictory information in the relevant literature. The description of size alone varies from five inches (Rutgers) to five and one-half (de Grahl) to six inches (Pinter). Even in Forshaw's work, otherwise considered scientifically accurate, there is only vague information concerning their natural life style, and the information referring to breeding habits is based on the observation of captive birds.

A. pullaria shows a wide distribution, living mainly on flat grassy steppes and the edges of light forestation. Grass seeds are their main staple, but berries and fruit, particularly wild figs, are also eaten. To the regret of the human population, red-faced lovebirds often devour entire millet fields; they know how to climb the stalks and how to descend head first!

As a nesting site, they prefer termite mounds, in which the walls consist of leaves which the termites glued together into a rigid cork-like mass. Into this, the females alone (the males participate only by singing) dig a tunnel, which ends in a fist-sized hollow. For nesting material they collect only leaves and small pieces of bark. There is no need to build a tube- or bowl-shaped nest, as do the previously cited species. The size of the clutch varies from two to seven eggs. The female alone incubates them for about twenty-two days. The young are covered with gray down. After four to six weeks,

The blue carpal edge of the wing is visible on this red-faced male.

This red-faced lovebird shows a distinct red patch in the tail.

Red-faced lovebirds prefer to nest in arboreal termitaria. A terrestrial termitarium is shown here.

they leave the nest. In juvenile plumage the males can be distinguished by the black undersides of their wings (green in females). The red face-mask is yellowish in the young of both sexes. In their mature plumages, the males and females of red-faced lovebirds are easily distinguished, because the females are slightly paler in all their colors. In Uganda there is a subspecies that differs slightly in color (paler) and size (larger): *A. p. ugandae.*

Hampe has mentioned the endurance and lack of susceptibility to cold of the species kept in northern latitudes, once the birds have been carefully acclimated; all other authorities emphasize a need for warmth and the general delicateness of the species in captivity. Even in regard to their diet, the information of the various authors differs considerably. Hampe and Pinter refer to a varied diet: in addition to a good exotic mixture, fruit, ant eggs and mealworm larvae should be given (hemp and sunflower seeds are rarely accepted). Rutgers complains that red-faced lovebirds will often eat only millet. Unfortunately, this matter may become insignificant because red-faced lovebirds are rarely obtainable commercially. Though comparatively inexpensive and frequently available after the last war, this species is absent from the market at present. It is possible, however, that this is due to a lack of demand. The word has spread that *A. pullaria* are not as easily kept and simply cannot be bred sufficiently under human care. Thus it would certainly be irresponsible to increase the number of birds taken from their already endangered environment. This is very unfortunate for the bird lover, because red-faced lovebirds are charming companions, lovable and lively in manner, quite tame with patient training, and—above all—not as raucous as their (probably not very close) relatives. Their song is pleasant chirping, their plumage colorful, and the sexes are easily distinguishable.

If any of our readers should still own red-faced lovebirds, or if the species should once more become available in the market, it will be helpful to have the few known facts about successful and attempted breeding in captivity. Around 1900, a successful attempt was made in Germany in an ordinary nesting box, but further details are not available. Hampe mentions a pair which in 1937 fed each other, mated repeatedly, and attempted to dig a tunnel into the stucco wall of their aviary after ignoring ordinary nesting boxes and a special concrete cave. The female persisted in loosening the mortar in one place until finally, with the help of the breeder, a sufficiently large cavity was formed. In it, the female built a nest of willow twigs, which she carried in her feathers. She laid and incubated five eggs, which were either not fertilized or contained dead embryos. In 1957, limited success was attained in England and by Hampe in Germany. In England, peat moss had been stuffed into hanging barrels and nesting cavities scooped out. Almost all of the fifteen pairs in this specially equipped aviary bred, but only one healthy youngster survived. In Germany, Hampe took the trouble of erecting a clay wall, into which a female dug a cavity by herself. One young bird hatched but did not survive. In Capetown, successful attempts involved very large aviaries containing only single pairs. The installations included large nest boxes filled with cork blocks and hung in tree branches. Two-inch holes were bored into the cork (de Grahl; no further information). In Switzerland, there was finally one successfull breeding after four years of failure with the same pair (de Grahl).

When comparing and evaluating these facts, so widely separated in time and space, one thing becomes evident: the female needs to dig her own nest into porous but not-too-loose material, accompanied by the male ready for mating. Only this will trigger their breeding instinct. The low incidence of hatching and the high mortality of the babies may well be caused by lack of experience. If there were more breeding attempts, more red-faced lovebirds in the possession of breeders, it would be possible to discover the elements lacking in their diet and care. In the absence of nest boxes, red-faced lovebirds have been said to occasionally sleep hanging upside down in the manner of hanging parrots *(Loriculus* species).

The basic seed mix of lovebird diets should be supplemented by fruits, greens, and soft foods, according to the birds' preferences. Shown is a peach-faced lovebird.

Above and opposite: Abyssinian lovebirds, *A. taranta*. The birds having the red coloring on the forehead and around the *eyes* are males.

Abyssinian Lovebird
Agapornis taranta

This largest species of lovebird (six and one-half inches) is at home in the wild mountains of Ethiopia, to an altitude of 9,000 feet. For this reason, they readily survive our winters in outdoor aviaries with an attached, unheated enclosed room. One requirement, of course, is careful acclimation. The difference in altitude may cause more problems for the birds than the change of temperature. Hampe cites an instance of a pair kept at liberty which began to breed in November at a temperature of around 40°F. In a starling box they hatched four healthy youngsters in mid winter at temperatures of about 25°F. It goes without saying that this should remain an exception and winter breeding should be avoided if possible.

The natural habitat of Abyssinian, or black-winged, lovebirds lies along the edges of evergreen mountain forests of the Abyssinian plateau, from where they descend, according to Forshaw, only when the figs are ripe, in small groups of up to ten birds. Despite a short flight distance, they rarely approach human habitations. This species nests singly, not in colonies, in hollow trees and knotholes. It does not appear to have a clearly defined breeding season. The females carry twigs and bark as nesting material, usually between the feathers of the chest and rump, but occasionally in their beaks. They simply put down a layer of these materials in a hollow, into which they lay three to five eggs, rarely six. The female incubates alone for twenty-four to twenty-five days, during which she is fed by the male. The hatch-

Above and opposite: Abyssinian lovebirds (males). It is likely that Abyssinian lovebirds can become accustomed to being kept at liberty.

lings are covered with white fuzz, which later changes to gray. They leave the nest at six to eight weeks and immediately fly quite well; nevertheless, the male continues to feed them for a few more weeks. There are no data available on successive breedings, if any. Their diet consists of several grass and tree seeds and fruit, although they are said to particularly enjoy bitter juniper berries.

The first Abyssinian lovebirds were imported to Austria in 1906, with a first breeding success in Vienna in 1911. In 1923, they were imported to England and from there in larger numbers to Germany. According to Pinter, some imported birds proceeded to breed successfully after only eight months. Altogether, this species cannot be considered easy to breed successfully, and it has never been very popular, despite many endearing qualities (it probably was never widely available on the market, either). It is possible that only the larger form *A. t. taranta* was imported, because there is no mention of the much smaller *A. t. nana* in the cited reports on care and breeding.

Some of the positive qualities of the Abyssinian lovebird have just been mentioned. To these must be added the fact of easy sex determination after the very first feathers have grown. The young males have wings black on the underside, while in the same place the females first are greenish, later gray-black. Many male fledglings already show the red eye rings, and the first red feathers on the head begin to sprout a little later, even though full coloration is not reached until about nine months of age. The birds are quiet and almost modest, uttering only an occasional soft chirping.

Their diet should be similar to that of the species with eye rings, with perhaps more sunflower seeds, only they need not be the white or striped kind. With their strong beaks, the Abyssinian lovebirds manage to open even the cheaper, black kind. They prefer fruit, such as apples and pears, to greens, but should be offered both. They also enjoy eating the bark of willow twigs; in winter, figs are the greatest delicacy.

Even though they are not susceptible to cold, summer is the best breeding time because of the availability of sun, greens, and fruit. Abyssinian lovebirds need slightly larger nesting boxes, which according to Rutgers should measure 11 by 4 by 12 inches high. It is best to place an inch-and-one-half of peat moss or coarse sawdust and woodshavings into the boxes, since not all females collect nesting materials. For this reason also, the floor should have a slight hollow. It is nevertheless recommended to have available moss, dry leaves of non-

Abyssinian lovebird male. This species is also known as the black-winged lovebird.

poisonous trees, and tree bark for those females who wish to construct a nest, according to Rutgers. Pinter mentions that some females do construct even quite elaborate nests.

Hand-raised Abyssinians become exceptionally tame and affectionate. I once saw a male who rode through the entire house and out onto the terrace on his owner's shoulder without leaving her.

The greatest drawback of these pleasant birds is their quarrelsomeness. Their quiet demeanor is misleading; they suddenly attack another bird's legs and will not let go, so that they often kill smaller birds and seriously injure larger ones. Unfortunately, this can also happen at the mesh separating aviaries. For this reason, a double wall of wire mesh at a distance of a couple of inches is recommended. We must strictly enforce the keeping of only one pair per aviary. Only parakeets larger than crimson rosellas whom they cannot hurt may be used as companions, one pair of each. Even cockatiels and red-rumped parrots have had their legs bitten, according to de Grahl. Because of the unpredictable behavior of the Abyssinians, their own young should be removed as soon as they are self-sufficient.

Unfortunately, Abyssinians have a more pronounced proclivity for feather plucking than any of the other lovebirds, whether their own or those of other birds, and even the down of their nestlings, which may lead to torn skin and death. One authority recommends giving the birds diatomaceous earth combined with vitamins to prevent further plucking as a result of some deficiency. Otherwise, the picked-on youngsters will have to be put into a separate cage within the parents' aviary, so that the adults will have to feed them through the wire, which they will usually do quite readily. Of course, the young must have reached about the age where they can survive on their own, because otherwise they will catch cold too easily.

Hampe succeeded in having Abyssinian babies raised by budgerigars, although only as long as they were in the nest, and after the young budgies were removed. After fledging, however, they were no longer fed by the budgerigars; until they were self-sufficient they had to be fed a gruel by means of a feeding syringe.

Above and opposite: gray-headed
lovebirds, *A. cana*. The coloration of
the male is the source of the name of
this dimorphic species.

Gray-headed Lovebird
Agapornis cana

As different as they may appear at first sight, these little island inhabitants only five inches long are the closest relatives of *A. taranta* mentioned above. When observed closely, a visible similarity is found in the darkness of the tips of the tail feathers in both species. More similarities are shown in their behavior. Both breed singly in hollow trees, and both usually carry their sparse nesting materials of dried or evergreen leaves tucked between the feathers on the rump. In the pertinent literature, both species are said to occasionally build elaborate nests in the manner of the lovebirds with eye rings. In both species, male and females remain faithfully together and except for the breeding season band together with others in small to medium-sized flocks. In captivity, they remain quite shy and will always be unpleasant and aggressive towards other species of birds.

Gray-headed lovebirds, found on the island of Madagascar and its neighbors, appear in two geographically isolated subspecies. In the southwest of Madagascar, the species *A. c. ablectanea* occurs. It is distinguished from *A. c. cana* by a more bluish hue to its plumage, with the males showing a purer and more extensive gray.

Outside of the breeding season these birds often roam about in flocks of varying sizes, doing considerable damage to the rice fields. They are noisy and lively but would rather not cross large open areas. They like to rest huddled closely together in date palms along the way. Their flight is curved, not straight as that of the other species of lovebirds. Their flight distance is con-

The natural range of the gray-headed
lovebird is confined to the island of
Madagascar; thus this species has
been called the Madagascar lovebird.

Opposite:
The line of demarcation between gray head and green
back is especially crisp in this
male specimen of *A. cana*.

siderable; that is, they are quite shy, even in the wild. Grass seeds, their main staple, are picked from the ground, where the birds walk about with rapid movements. They are said to associate on their foraging trips with weaver finches of the *Lonchura* or the thick-billed species. On some of the smaller islands off the east coast of Africa, as well as on the coast, *A. cana* are said to have been introduced but have died out (Forshaw). Other islands they colonized by themselves and can still be found there.

The usual number of eggs in a clutch is three or four, occasionally as many as seven. Incubation lasts for eighteen to twenty-two days. The young leave the nest at five to six weeks, fully feathered. In the wild the young males are said to be pure green when they leave the nest and indistinguishable from the females; in captivity, they clearly show the gray head and neck, even though somewhat diluted. Similar instances of bypassing the juvenile plumage in captivity are known in other species of birds, but as yet there are no plausible explanations for this phenomenon. Young gray-heads attain their full adult coloration at four to five months.

From 1872 on, gray-heads were imported in large numbers, and the first breeding success occurred in Germany in that same year. Nevertheless, they were never considered good and reliable breeders. In the beginning, nobody bothered much with breeding, since the imported supply was always so abundant that the birds were even available for sale in department stores. Unfortunately, during those years, much damage was done to these lovely parrots, partly through ignorance, partly through carelessness. This changed only later, after World War II and several years without imports. The birds became much rarer and therefore more expensive. Today their exportation from Madagascar is prohibited. Consequently, it is a considerable success that domestically bred gray-headed lovebirds are once again exhibited at all major shows. It is doubtful, however, whether the present domestic stock is sufficient to ensure the future of the species in captivity.

These birds are not suited for everyone: love, patience, and a suitable installation are essential. Although Rutgers bred them in small cages only sixty inches long, they exhibit fright and boredom in close quarters; they do not act naturally, but screech loudly when approached and disappear into the box. Without nest boxes, they are even less happy, huddle in the farthest corner, and so on. The most suitable arrangement calls for fairly large indoor aviaries with connected, smaller outdoor flights. While imported gray-heads

Above: gray-headed lovebird female. Opposite: the coloration indicates this is a young gray-headed male.

need to be kept warm in a heated environment in the winter, at least until acclimated, those bred in captivity are hardier and can withstand colder temperatures, but they must be protected from frost and damp drafts. Since the gray-heads do not get along with each other and the females especially fight over nesting boxes, each pair should have its own small aviary, if possible. A particularly peaceable and close pair, though, can often share a bigger aviary with peaceable species of large parakeets.

As soon as gray-heads are able to maintain their flight distance, they become more pleasant and can be bred successfully. Roomy budgerigar nest boxes are preferred, with a layer of sawdust or peat moss. The birds are not choosey about nesting material, but they tend to amass empty millet sprays. Gray-heads have an interesting mating behavior. The males dance around the females, which often hang upside down from nesting boxes to indicate their readiness to breed; this makes perches a necessity.

Many parents resent checking of the nest box. In order to band the babies, it is recommended to remove the parents from the nest box by means of some favorite tidbit. When banding, the rings should be pushed over the front toes to the joint, and the back toe pulled gently through the ring by means of a flattened stick. The best time for banding is usually on about the twelfth day, but experience will be the best teacher, from case to case and species to species.

Dry (even better, germinated) spray millet is their favorite delicacy. Their diet should be the same as that for other small lovebirds. Since not all gray-heads like greens, they should become accustomed quite early to a conditioning food that includes grated carrots.

It is possible to keep these species at liberty during the summer, if the partners have first become used to flying in and out singly. De Grahl says that domestically bred gray-heads showed no discomfort at 16°F., but such experiments are not recommended with this species, as it is quite rare today. These birds cannot survive a winter in the open.

A hand-raised youngster even learned to repeat a few words, according to Hampe. Gray-headed lovebirds which will be exhibited should be trained to the show cages carefully from earliest youth, since otherwise they tend to fuss loudly and assume stiff and unnatural poses.

Opposite, clockwise: red-faced male, Abyssinian male, black-collared male *A. s. swinderniana*, black-collared male *A. s. zenkeri*, gray-headed male, gray-headed female (reproduced from Forshaw, *Parrots of the World*). Below: black-collared lovebird, a mounted specimen.

Black-collared Lovebird
Agapornis swinderniana

The natural range of black-collared lovebirds is so large that three geographic races are distinguished, yet less is known about them than about any other lovebirds. According to the literature, these lovebirds have never been brought to Europe and were caged, unsuccessfully, only once in the Congo. There, they would only eat fig seeds, and only if offered in whole fresh figs. Yet an analysis of their stomach contents shows that these birds eat other fruits as well, and also millet, half-ripe corn, insect larvae, and caterpillars. Theoretically, it should be possible with modern nutritional science to hand-feed them with a nourishing, protein-rich diet by means of a feeding syringe put directly into the crop until they are willing to accept germinated Senegal millet or similar small seed.

Unfortunately, there are no black-collared lovebirds available on the market. My personal friend and noted German lovebird breeder, Siegfried Bischoff, on his own initiative undertook an expedition in 1979 to their natural habitat to find out more about them. He only saw—and even that is not quite certain—several birds fly by at a distance. Therefore, we can only reproduce a picture, not a color photograph. Yet Swindern's lovebirds have been known since 1820, according to Hampe. They measure five to six inches and are the only species whose habitat is the dense tropical forest, to an altitude of about 6,000 feet. From there, small flocks of fifteen to twenty birds are said to make excursions to neighboring grain fields, but mostly they remain in the dense forest canopy, rarely descending to the ground.

As mentioned previously, their preferred food seems to be fresh fig seeds, which they pick from the ripe fruit; yet even in the fertile tropical climate, these are not available year round, which leads us to believe that the birds must eat other things too.

It is quite possible that black-collared lovebirds are often overlooked because of their soft coloring and soft voices. Therefore, the estimates concerning their numbers are very vague, and observations of breeding habits are practically nonexistent. Neither nests nor eggs have been described. It can only be assumed that they breed in tree cavities in July, since males with fully developed gonads were captured in July, according to Forshaw. Thus, these birds offer an exciting challenge to explorers!

According to Hampe, the *A. s. zenkeri* differs from *A. s. swinderniana* by a wide orange-to-red-brown neckband. Their range is the former Cameroons. *A. s. emini* is larger, with a coarser, hooked beak. They occur in the central Congo and western Uganda, isolated from *A. s. zenkeri* geographically.

Perhaps it will be possible one day to capture and import these elusive birds and to get to know them after successful importation and acclimation. Until then, lovebird fanciers have the happy task of caring for all the other *Agapornis* species in order to preserve them for future generations, independent of further importation. This is particularly true of the many species which are presently endangered: *A. nigrigenis, A. lilianae, A. taranta,* and, above all, *A. pullaria,* whose domestic numbers have shrunk alarmingly.

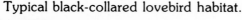
Typical black-collared lovebird habitat.

Index

Page numbers in parentheses refer to illustrations.

Abyssinian lovebird, 63-68; (9, 10, 27, 62, 63, 64, 65, 66)

African savannah, (8)

Agapornis cana, 69-74

Agapornis cana ablectanea, 69

Agapornis fischeri, 31-34

Agapornis lilianae, 35-38

Agapornis nigrigenis, 39-40

Agapornis personata, 17-30

Agapornis pullaria, 57-62

Agapornis pullaria ugandae, 60

Agapornis roseicollis, 43-56

Agapornis roseicollis catumbella, 43

Agapornis swinderniana, 75-76

Agapornis swinderniana emini, 76

Agapornis swinderniana zenkeri, 76

Agapornis taranta, 63-68

Agapornis taranta nana, 66

Aggression, 32, 46, 67, 69, 73

Atavism, 14

Banding, 29, 73

Black-cheeked lovebird, 39-40; (9, 10, 38, 39, 40; yellow, 10)

Black-collared lovebird, 75-76; (6, 74, 75)

Black-collared lovebird habitat, (76)

Blue varieties, 28, 36, 47, 52-55

Bordered varieties, 52-53

Breeding behavior, 9-10, 14, 21, 25, 28, 31-32, 35, 39-40, 43, 46-47, 52-54, 57, 60-61, 63

Budgerigar (parakeet), 28-29, 47, 52-55, 67

Cinnamon varieties, 52-53

Color varieties, 14, 28, 32, 40, 47, 52-54

Cork, 60

Dark factor, 54

Dark green varieties, 53-55

Diatomaceous earth, 67

Dilute varieties, 52-53

Distribution map, (11)

Double-wiring, 67

Egg binding, 46

Eggs, 9, 24, 35, 46, 57, 63, 72; (23)

Exhibiting, 29, 40

Feather-plucking, 67

Feeding, 10, 22-23, 32, 36, 40, 46, 57, 60, 66, 73, 75

Fischer's lovebird, 31-34; (26, 30, 31, 33)

Golden Cherry mutation, 52

Gray-headed lovebird, 69-74; (10, 26, 68, 69, 70, 71, 72, 73)

Hand-raising, 18, 21, 67, 73, 75

Houseplants, poisonous, 18

Housing, 17, 21-25, 32, 36, 40, 46, 60, 63, 67, 72

Humidity, 46

Hybrids, 13-14, 28, 39

Incubation, 9, 24, 35, 46, 57, 63, 72

Illness, 21

Import-export, 10, 39, 46, 60, 66, 72, 75

Inbreeding, 14, 32

Liberty, keeping at, 40, 55, 73

Lonchura species, 72

Loriculus species, 61

Loss mutation, 32

Lutino varieties, 36, 52

Masked lovebird, 17-30; (7, 16, 17, 24, 26, 29, 41; blue, 9, 20, 25, 26, 27; blue-white, 19; yellow, 19; orange, 22)

Mauve varieties, 53-55

Nesting, 17-18, 22, 24, 41, 46, 57, 60-61, 63, 66, 69, 73

Nest box, (15)

Nestlings, 21, 24, 46, 72

Nyasa lovebird, 35-38; (9, 12, 34, 35, 37; lutino, 47)

Olive varieties, 53-55

Peat, 60, 66

Peach-faced lovebird, 43-56; (15, 23, 26, 27, 41, 42, 50, 51, 61; albino, 49, 52; blue, 27, 45, 49, 52; dilute blue, 46; dilute yellow-green, 44; Golden Cherry, 52; lutino, 9, 54; pastel-blue, 9; pied yellow-green, 9, 52, 55; red-flecked, 10, 53; yellow, 43, 47, 48, 49)

Pets, lovebirds as, 18-21, 67, 73

Pied varieties, 31, 47, 53

Red-faced lovebird, 57-62; (10, 56, 57, 58, 59)

Scaled varieties, 52

Sexing, 23, 43, 66

Temperature tolerance, 14, 18, 21, 24, 35, 39, 40, 47, 63, 73

Termitaria, 57; (59)

Voice, 18, 31, 36, 43, 60, 76

Water, 10, 22

White varieties, 28

Yellow varieties, 28, 31, 32, 52

Yellow-green varieties, 52